LETTERS ON ART AND LITERATURE

LETTERS ON ART AND LITERATURE

FRANÇOIS MAURIAC

PHILOSOPHICAL LIBRARY
NEW YORK

15 East 40th Street, New York 16, N. Y.

Translated from the French *Lettres Ouvertes*
by Mario A. Pei

ISBN 978-0-8065-2900-4

Printed in the United States of America

I

AFTER THE DEATH OF GEORGES BERNANOS

You have taken it upon yourself to write me, Sir, taking me to task for the fact that I kept silent when Georges Bernanos died. You pretend to believe that it was a low spirit of resentment that kept me from paying him the homage I owed him. On the one hand, you do me the honor of believing that I could have said about him things that escaped most of those who wrote in his praise; but on the other hand, you don't believe that I am capable of forgetting insults: "Especially," you add, "those that Bernanos heaped upon you, which perhaps shocked some readers of *L'Intransigeant*, but delighted a far greater number."

You remind me that in *Figaro* (which Bernanos, in one of his last articles, compared to a house of ill-repute), M. André Rousseaux did not hesitate to proclaim that so far as he is concerned, he never deemed his judicial fits of anger excessive. That is not going far enough. If *Figaro's* critic had been entirely sincere, he would have confessed that this anger delighted him more than anything else in Bernanos.

Note that in this connection André Rousseaux gives way to what I may call a Sainte-Beuve complex. Following the example of this illustrious critic, he judges himself far superior in experience and knowledge to those of his contemporaries who have arrived and rest secure in their success. Too often, in a man of intellect whose task it is to judge other people's books, envy, that most ignoble of passions, is confused with a feeling of offended justice. Perhaps dear Rousseaux, in order to help himself live, has tucked away in some secret drawer, like Sainte-Beuve, secret notebooks filled with different poisons. But what good are these posthumous pleasures which we can enjoy only in advance, and of which our ashes will know nothing? The truth is that the fury of Bernanos pleased our friend Rousseaux by reason of an excess of that bitterness which imparts to everything he writes a rich jaundiced color. A great writer may think he is only venting his own spleen; but actually he may also serve as an outlet for less illustrious spleens; in this way, Bernanos did much good to many people.

Coming back to your letter, don't you think, Sir, that if I had dedicated to Georges Bernanos, the one of my contemporaries whom I perhaps most admired, the article which I alone, true enough, could have written about him (not necessarily better than others, but nevertheless irreplaceable), you would have written me a very similar letter, in which, however, you would have reproached me for taking advantage of the silence of a once mighty personage, now dead and therefore unable to speak in his own defense? However, know this: a man like Bernanos never passed on his colleagues, and particularly on me, an unequivocal judgment. In this respect we are all alike. There is something we hate in those we love, and something we like in our worst enemies; it is simply a matter of letting the light fall on one side or the other. So far as I am concerned, Bernanos often shifted the lamp. I am no collector of old papers, but without going into extensive research I can give you two examples which, I have no doubt, will come as a great surprise to you. If I were to go through my files I could certainly find others, but these, I think, will suffice. As you first glance at these texts, I fear you will accuse me of yielding to vanity, or at least to a sense of pride. Far from it: if you have the patience to read this letter to the end, you will see that on the contrary I have only sought to throw some light, for your sake and my own, on the reasons why Bernanos was at every turn offended and irritated by my sort of Christian.

That he did me justice on the political plane you

may gather from this dedication which he inscribed on my copy of *Grands Cimetières sous la lune*: "This book can enter only through the breach which you have so courageously and so nobly opened. May you not find it too unworthy of you! With all my admiration, and all my heart."

But there is a more explicit text that touches the heart of the matter. I quote from one of the last letters I received from him, undated, but subsequent to the Liberation. After outlining his reasons (none of them offensive to the Academy), why he did not wish to sit in that body, he adds: "It seems to me that many matters would be cleared up between us if only we knew each other better; but it also seems to me that in spite of the many things that draw us together, your youthful approach to life and mine, in the distant past, were so differently slanted as to preclude our ever understanding each other completely, even though we may be in basic agreement. However, I know from experience how often your name is linked with mine by many of our overseas friends, who perhaps know better than we what we mean to each other. We therefore find ourselves united in their hearts, even while we wait to be better joined one day in the gentle mercy of God, as in an everlasting morning. Believe that I feel with you deeply."

You will admit, Sir, that the Bernanos who speaks here comes closer to the author of the *Journal d'un curé de campagne* than to the writer who claimed in *L'Intransigeant* to André Rousseaux's delight, that in my writings he heard and smelled the sounds and odors of a water-closet. But do not fear that I may wish to take up arms against you, or above all against the Georges Bernanos of this admirable text; the charity that here overflows (and charity was the very foundation of his nature, while insult was only a fringe of foam) certainly touches, strikes and humiliates me, but neither offends nor degrades me.

THE GOOD SHARP ARROW AND ITS ENDURING KEENNESS

The truth is that there are two kinds of Christians (by Christians I mean people who try to live according to Grace). The majority of them do not refuse to adapt themselves to a world beset by evil, or to come to terms with it. They fully understand what the great Bossuet meant when he confessed that he could do nothing well "if he was at odds with his servant." They don't seek out posts and honors, but they accept them when they are offered, first because nothing seems more exaggerated to them than certain spectacular refusals, second because they figure that the best way not to think about the *Institut* or similar things is to be part of them; Barrès has taught them, from their early youth, that we can be entirely sure of holding in contempt only the goods we actually possess, and these are also the only things we can truly renounce; for how is one to renounce what he does not have? (They remember in this connection the infinite importance that Péguy, for instance, attributed not merely to the Academy, but to one of the Grands Prix which he was so shamefully refused.) When these Christians grow old they realize too late that it does them no good to shake themselves, for the accoutrements of the world cling to their skins and keep them apart from that humble and living part of mankind which they cherish, and by which they would have wished to be understood and loved.

But above everything else, these settled and secure Christians collaborate in an order which is in essence unjust. Evil and the mystery of evil do not deter them from trying to be happy in accordance with the ways of the world. To them, evil appears under the guise of a problem that the theologians skilfully solve by their subtleties, with which secular Christians pretend to be satisfied. It is part of Georges Bernanos' greatness that he thought, wrote and suffered in the very center of this drama of a creation which was once redeemed by the Son of Man, but which is now once more losing itself. He, too, knew to his dying breath the temptation to yield to despair, which wears out saints. But he never lost the will to believe. What a faith was his! If you were to ask me what I admire most about him, I would say that it is his faith, the fact that he never doubted God's mercy, although he was face to face with evil; that his work bears witness to the love of the Creator for His creatures; that in this murderous world in which he lived (and in which we continue to live), where this divine love is insulted, rejected, held in contempt by many, and completely ignored by many more, he held fast; that he did not lose heart when for him holiness remained crucified on the very brink of despair. Yes, all this helps me to understand why, in these last years of his life, he turned into an old molossus with bloodshot eyes, biting at the shins of fat sheep and foolish ewes.

As for France, he confused her with the image he had in his heart; that of a young girl, almost a child, betrayed into the hands of the official Church and the Sorbonne; a little Jeanne d'Arc. He never ceased viewing us, whether we wore a pectoral cross, green robes or red robes, as scheming wild beasts who tortured and martyred a child after having first attempted to bring shame upon her. In his heart and mind, he never ceased to contrast this adored little girl with the France of today, such as it is, or rather, such as it seems to be, the France of the profiteers, a France whose richest vein may well turn out to be the trench in which lie rotting the bodies of those Resistance martyrs of all parties who faced the firing-squads.

That he erred against justice is self-evident: there survived in him something of the old *camelot du roi* who, at the mere mention of Christian Democracy, went into a fit of alarm. (We must face the fact that Charles Maurras, who supplied a ready-made system, a sort of "national costume" for ordinary minds, also left an indelible imprint on some very keen intellects, even among those most violently opposed to him. Notice, for instance, André Rousseaux, who is never so much a follower of Maurras as when he puffs up and labors to admire André Breton or Miller; he, whose youth was nurtured on the hills of moderation in the shadow of Massis and his rod, watch him forcing himself to chew up and swallow the dead fodder of surrealism!)

When all is said and done, it is upon our faith and the quality of our faith that a man like Bernanos compels us to examine ourselves. Was not that slightly demented manner of his the manner of a Christian who not only has a notional idea of the verities defined by the theologians, but lives them and suffers from them almost unto death? If Satan were to us this creature of whom Bernanos speaks as of someone whose breath he feels in his face, would we be able, any more than he was, to resign ourselves to the rules of the social game? Would we too not be overwhelmed by the ridiculousness of man without God, which perhaps surpasses the ridiculousness of man who believes himself to be with God?

After the Liberation, what party, what newspaper, what academy did not dream of adding to itself this great virgin force? But Bernanos made it clear to us that he did not belong to the world. He finally came to this conclusion after having sought for years, in a very simple fashion, I imagine, a retreat where he could breathe, live and taste a humble human happiness. For there was nothing of the ascetic in him. It took him some time to realize that he would not find a place of refuge in this world, that there was no place for him, that he belonged to the wandering race of inspired objectors. Nevertheless, "the note of Eden-like purity, of infinite gentleness, of heart-rending sadness" that Paul Claudel was the first to discern in Rimbaud is the same as the one that charms us in Bernanos. But while in *La Saison en enfer* it appears only at times, in the midst of the imprecations of an angry child, in Bernanos, whether shrill or muffled, it is sustained; and no cry of disgust ever masks it completely. Did he hold himself in less horror than he did us? Perhaps Bernanos took upon himself and bore in our place that unhappiness at not being a saint which hardly disturbs us.

You will admit, Sir, that I am far from feeling injured, as you thought I would be, by the caricatures of Christian Democrats and liberal journalists in which you think Bernanos excels. True, he is the novelist of the great inner void; he bears no resemblance to those novelists with monocles who "observe." Whatever opinion one may have of Christian Democracy, the modernistic and liberal worms that swarm in *L'Imposture,* for instance, give us no information save about Bernanos himself, just as the nightmare of a fever patient or a madman gives information to the psychiatrist. Bernanos comes close to Dostoievsky, who creates his own mental universe and fills it with creatures to his own image and likeness; not to Tolstoi, who rebuilds and brings back to life a world familiar to all of us. It is remarkable that even Bernanos' priests, despite their dazzling reality, resemble no living priest, and that no one, to my knowledge, finds that he resembles them. Those I have questioned on this matter, whether or not they admired Bernanos, have always rejected the idea that there was the least semblance of reality in his holy and terrible characters. Indeed, their disturbing presence is the presence of Bernanos himself, that priestly soul condemned to wander among us under the guise of a man of letters; for thirty years we have admired and loved from a distance that wild bird that hurled itself against the bars of a materialistic cage in which we all settled down as best we could, with the least inconvenience, and with that desire for comfort which no apocalyptic vision could discourage.

All of us? No, here I am yielding too much to the fascination of this intractable brother. Admit, Sir, that there are men for whom "living in accordance with one's period" involves no compromise; Bernanos' refusal to compromise, however noble it may seem to us, nevertheless partakes of a certain sterile pride. This inspired soul, who was able to create saints, infusing into them his own breath, was also able to transmit some elements of his own deep nature to creatures molded by hate. In the first pages of *L'Imposture* (one of his least successful books, but still my favorite, for the most peculiar qualities of beauty appear in it: the Abbé Cénabre stands out as the only great Luciferian figure in all our literature), you will recall that terrible priest torturing a little liberal journalist in the confessional; there is not a word uttered by this terrible abbé in which I do not recognize the voice, the accent, even the vocabulary of Bernanos when he was carried away by his emotions, and in which there does not vibrate a hatred as supernatural as is the admirable love which he retained until the very end.

But that is enough to put us on our guard. In spite of Bernanos' advice and all his words of execration, men must stay in their native land and consent to work in the mud; the seeds sown by generations of democratic priests, at whom he scoffed, have to bear their fruit in the byways; simple Christians must be willing to dirty their hands in politics, they must wear themselves out laboring in the holds of the dismantled ship so they may repair all the leaks in them. Let us not yield to the easy temptation of placing the real nation on the level of Joan of Arc, the holy curate of Ars, and Péguy, so that we may have the right to kick aside the other France, as though it were a rotting boat. The real France is the one of which we are a part. We may be ashamed of it in this long period of waiting, but we still want to look into its ravaged face with love. That is the France to which we choose to remain loyal, not the excessively sublime image that Bernanos holds up above our reach through the centuries and into the heavens.

You will reply that Bernanos hardly ran the risk of creating a school of followers, and you are right; that he was one of those men through whom a race, even when dishonored, preserves the consciousness of its mission, and I grant you that, too; that in the shadow of the huge materialistic beast that each day stretches farther over us, he remained, until death and after, a witness of the Love which is no longer loved, and here again I say that you are right.

Believe me, Sir, it pleases me to let you have the final word.

II

WHAT DO YOU EXPECT OF A PRIEST?

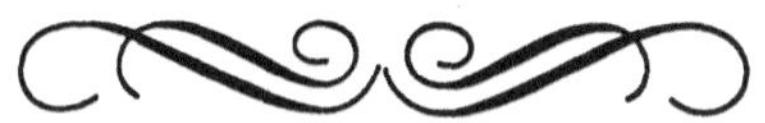

Your Reverence, I must confess that my first impulse was to crumple up your letter into a ball and throw it into the waste paper basket. "What does a priest mean to you?" you ask me. "What do you expect of a priest?" People who ask such questions, especially when they are canons, are extremely rash; they don't realize that they are helping to revive the custom of public confession. It is true that they address themselves specifically to men of letters whose trade it is to tell their life-story to every comer. Just how far the men of letters have gone in this direction since the days of Jean-Jacques can be seen today, when husbands publish household chronicles that elicit from their readers a laughter of disgust unknown to our fathers, while single men tell even more concisely what they do when they are alone. In fact, eroticism itself is surpassed by this love of self-abasement for its own sake. The erotic person does not take delight in what degrades him, because he does not feel degraded, while the self-abaser resembles the patient who eventually comes to love the smell of his own bandages.

You wonder, Your Reverence, what I am getting at? I am merely trying to say that like most of my colleagues I have done nothing all my life except to talk about myself; not, of course, in the direct fashion of those who discuss their wives, their vices, or their manias. Discretion, even prudence perhaps, are not heroic virtues. But who can definitely assert that a self-abaser does not possess a sort of corrupt virtue, or that we should not give him credit for this need he feels of being henceforth known for what he really is, this certainty he seems to crave that he is no longer fooling anyone? One might say that his corruption stems not from his confession, but rather from the pride he takes in it, and from his utilization of the worst and dirtiest qualities within him, which is the particular trick of the man of letters when he feels incapable of reinventing or even of transposing anything.

But is there not also a leaning toward exhibitionism in an author who chooses to describe his relations with God? Is self-edification in this case not merely a mask for the same kind of base desire? I am thus forced to admit that I have given you the right to ask me the question: "And what have you to say about this man in a black robe?" The answer to that question will be easy only to those who entered the Church at an adult age and by deliberate choice. But so far as I am concerned, priests have been a part of my life as far back as I can remember. My widowed mother followed their directions to the letter. My grandmother had in her garden a private chapel where Mass was celebrated, and there, amid the perfume of heliotropes and geraniums, during oppressive afternoons, I felt the little consecrated wafers coming to life; round about, to the child that I was then, stood a zone filled with burning silence.

To me, the priest goes on being what he was at the dawn of my life, but first and above all, he is the one who binds and releases, the one who, when he raises his hand to absolve us, can no longer be distinguished from the Son of Man to Whom was given the power to grant the remission of sins here on earth. This is a power which perhaps dazzles us most when we have no grave sin to confess, because it is then that the Grace attached to the Sacrament of Penance acts in its pure state, if I may dare say so, and that we feel it right down into our very flesh. Those who praise the Church for inventing the therapeutics of confession long in advance of Freud don't know what they are talking about. It is not the act of bringing our shameful deeds into the open that delivers us from them; it is a gesture, a word, a power. What does the priest mean to me? The meeting of the Power of God and the weakness of a mortal being in one and the same person. At this point, I shall confide to you a great grace that I have received, and if I am to believe many confidences, it is not a common one: although I have known many priests since the day I was born, I have never yet met one who scandalized me or did any evil; but I have known many who edified me, and several who, at certain turning points in my life, carried me on their shoulders. On this subject I have some memories that I share with God alone, because the priest himself will never know what grace he has transmitted until the evening when, as a poor worker, standing worn and exhausted on the threshold of eternal joy, he will be amazed at the words he hears and the reward that is vouchsafed him.

The priest, who grants the remission of sins, consecrates the Host for me. You say that he does the same for everybody: "But for you in particular, what is he?" Nothing more than what I am telling you: he is the one who, after pardoning me, puts the Host in my mouth; the one who, before giving it to me, elevates it for a moment above the ciborium.

Neither in my mind nor in my heart can I separate even a mediocre priest from this act which he performs every morning, this offering from God to God and from God to Man, who receives the Sacrament—a man who is often I.

Dare I confess to you now what I erroneously do not expect of a priest? I ask him only to give me God, not to talk to me of God. I do not underestimate the value of the ministry of words, but after all you are inquiring about my own particular needs. To me, a priest's most effective sermon has always been his own life. A good priest has nothing to tell me. I look at him, and that is enough. The liturgy that suffices for me is a silent sermon. The Religious Order that speaks most effectively of God are the Benedictines, because they never ascend the pulpit, but make the drama of the Mass live for us and reveal to us its daily sublime value. How well I understand what Kierkegaard means when he writes that God is someone to Whom we speak, not someone we speak about! How I pity the Protestants, whose cult is limited to preaching! Holy liturgy is the only preaching that touches and persuades me. There is no preacher with whom, from his third sentence, I do not disagree. The sacred orator seems equally formidable to me, be he eloquent or not. There are exceptions? To be sure! One of them makes me rejoice every Sunday on the broadcast of the Mass: Father Avril and the other Father who sometimes replaces him; and it is a joy to me to think how many thousands of people are listening to them.

In a word, Your Reverence, what is a priest to me? He is Christ. What do I expect of a priest, and what do I receive from him? Christ. He gives me Christ in His power, but he also shows me Christ in His suffering. In the twilight of my life I can say that I understand what a priest suffers; not so much, as one might expect, during the first years of his ministry, because youth, in one who is chosen, is the time for giving of oneself to the point of folly; but in the maturity of age, at the hour of fatigue, disillusionment and rebuffs, the priest often feels in his human heart regret for the humble human happiness he has given up, especially children. It is always the children of others, never his own. When one stops to think of it, what a miracle it is that so many thousands of men and women consent to make this sacrifice, which they pass on from generation to generation, and that most of them bear this cross right up to the end without flinching! I remember the young sister of Saint Vincent de Paul (she has since died at her work) who, watching my children at play, suddenly said to my wife in a tone I shall never forget: "How lucky you are, Madame!" And I reread the letters written to me by that vicar of Notre-Dame de Plaisance, Rémy Pasteau, killed by the enemy on Pentecost Day in 1940: ". . . All the fatigue that one must bear from morning to night, the overwhelming labor of a parish, of catechisms, of works. . . . And lately, convoys, nearly every day: a horror so strong that I can scarcely pray or keep up, at least externally, a semblance of the compassionate attitude these poor people need so much. I want to believe that in this fashion I have taken on myself, as often before, the hardest trials of someone dear to me; I want to believe that no part of this is useless. I live without any further hope, because trust is not hope. . . ."

Bernanos' country priest? Yes, of course. But the holiness of the little vicar of the ordinary type is not that sort: he eats black bread, and no angel comes to wipe the sweat from his brow. The true drama of the priest has never yet been written. The sinner unburdens himself to him as if he were God Himself, as if the priest were not himself a tempted and bruised human being. How many times is he besought to give out the strength of which he feels himself bereft, to preach a love whose flickering flame his will alone keeps alive within him! He never has the right to throw up the sponge or to quit the game, even for a minute.

Do canons read *Masses Ouvrières,* the review of the J.O.C.? I do. There is much food for thought in confidences like this one, in the November issue: "The atmosphere of a certain number of parishes tragically puts to the test the perseverance of young vicars in that priestly and pastoral ideal which was theirs when they left the seminary." Do you sometimes read, Your Reverence, these letters signed "a vicar"? Are you sensitive, as I am, to this complaint of being alone with God, uttered by a young and consecrated human being? "I find myself alone before a task that is new to me. Alone with Christ, true; but just the same, there are moments when one loses one's footing, when one feels the need of a visible aid. . . . If only our curés gave us confidence!"

What is the priest to me? Your Reverence, I always think of a living or dead priest when I despair of man, and the temptation to sin by contempt has me by the throat. Basically, and without being conscious of it, priests are the only true poets, the only ones who have made a positive choice. Far more than Rimbaud and all the idols of today's youth, they have set themselves apart from the world. They are the only ones who, by consenting to receive this sign for all eternity, have burned all their bridges behind them. What if some of them do falter? It removes from them nothing of the value of the gesture they once made, when they prostrated themselves face to the ground, on the day they gave themselves up. What if there are mediocre priests, which I grant you—all those whom we see unfortunately using the great power they have received in such indifferent manner that a layman could just as well replace them? Nor do I forget the bureaucratic-minded priests who push themselves ahead. And there are especially those most unfortunate of all men, the priests who have lost their faith in the power that brings us to their knees, and who are prisoners of something which is to them no longer anything but a myth, wearing a mask that they must constantly put back in place, men whose incurably blessed hands are forever stretched out toward the object of their covetousness. But what a narrow idea we have of the "bad priest" in Catholic circles! How little it takes to make us pin this label on those who struggle, fall and rise again! How strict are our requirements with respect to them! How presumptuous we are in thus anticipating the judgment of God! A Catholic writer, in the evening of his life, knows very well that he is himself redeemed by the same mercy, and that there is no way of separating his case from theirs.

Jacques Maritain once wrote that the responsibility

of a man of letters is such that if he is a Christian he must push faith to the point of folly. I know a writer who has not attained this degree of folly, who has not become literally mad with confidence, and this because he well knows that every morning more than one poor curé, in his deserted church, remembers his name at the point in the Consecration when it is no longer the priest who lives, but Christ who lives in the priest. Yes, I know that at that moment my name is tenderly uttered in a low voice.

You have induced me, Your Reverence, to reveal what should be buried deepest in a man's soul, because to such secrets as these, perhaps, can be applied the words of the Apostle concerning the mysteries of self-abasement: "Let there never be any question of it amongst you. . . ." At any rate, thanks to your questions, I have been able to bear witness to the many good and holy priests I have known; and for that I thank you.

III

TO ALBERT CAMUS

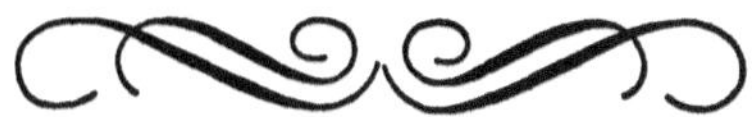

"Answers to an Unbeliever" is the title of an article in *Combat* which you, Albert Camus, have written to convince me that I was wrong in not going along with Garry Davis, the conscientious objector. For a long time I have been pondering over the strange fact that in your opinion I am the unbeliever and you are the believer. Is it possible that the impulse that draws you into the following of this little man is of a religious nature? Did I, in this particular instance, yield to the bitterness I have often felt toward those who are so quick to follow every newcomer, but invariably say no to the Son of Man?

But this train of thought would carry me too far from the subject and put me on dangerous ground, where I would again risk arousing your mistrust. How difficult it is for us to get together in our minds! How much more difficult it is for one generation to speak to another! Every time I have met you, every time we have dined together, after a few minutes of embarrassment you have accepted me as a friend, like all others. We have spoken freely, and at times I was even able to get a laugh out of you. But the very next day you would again retreat to a safe distance, that insurmountable distance that separates those who are coming from those who are leaving. I have had leisure to think of these things ever since I have attained what I call "the age of the coconut tree." Do you know what I mean by that? I mean the age when the old man clings to the palm branches and from his perch watches the young cannibals below; a position made all the more dangerous by the fact that he wears a two-cornered hat and his legs keep getting all tangled up in his sword. I may add that he has to struggle against a mighty temptation to rain down coconuts on those young heads all bristling with the headdress launched by Cocteau as far back as 1917; because, after all, many of your comrades have taken nearly everything from that distant period, even the haircut!

But reassure yourself. I am through joking. I am aware that this controversy outstrips our own individual destiny, and that it is the destiny of mankind that is at stake. As you said in the fine text published in *La Gauche,* every word of which aroused in me a profound echo, "there is no life without discussion." A discussion, not a controversy, is what we should henceforth try to carry on. I wish you might understand how close we are to each other, or, if you prefer, how close I feel to you. Above all, do not fear that as a Christian I shall try to convert you to my way of thinking. To tell the truth, you are the very type of man Saint Augustine had in mind when he used the words *anima naturaliter christiana.* I do not say this in order to compromise you, but only to justify, if need be, the trust with which I tell you of my doubts and difficulties on this subject, on which, it seems, we are divided. If I were only trying to be brilliant at any cost and to steal the show from you, I would no doubt seek the holes in your armor. But that's not the issue. What I have to do is to get down to cases and find out, along with you and helped by you, just where I stand on this problem that none of us can any longer avoid.

Since you recognized at first glance the strength of my position, and since you could not deny that the action of Garry Davis could benefit the propaganda of only one side of the world, strengthening Stalin's hand with an unhoped-for card, you by-passed this obstacle, and engaging in a counter-attack, you listed the consequences of the decision I was making: according to you, I would find myself bound hand and foot and delivered over to the United States on the international plane, to Gaullism on the national; I would have to support the cold war, fight a battle to the death with the Communists, approve of the policy of repression in Greece, and become reconciled with Franco. Since time admittedly works in Russia's favor, I would even have to be converted to the idea of a preventive war.

But you are quite wrong, my dear Camus. All these prospects shock me quite as much as they shock you. I reject the dilemma in which you place me. Fundamentally, this is my idea: I no longer believe that there are solutions of a sentimental nature in politics. I am positive that in the end they always carry grist to the enemy's mill. This does not mean that I incline to the side of force. Jacqueline Pascal said she entered Port-Royal because there one could rationally work out one's salvation. I hold that a rational policy that would take into account nothing but the facts could still save our generation from the atomic menace.

Perhaps it astonishes and shocks you that a Catholic should speak in this fashion. But it is precisely the Christian in me that refuses any longer to turn away from the evidence that all human politics is criminal by nature, or rather, since the idea of crime implies the idea of responsibility, that it is as amoral as the instinct of leopards and tigers. If you push me further along this road and ask me what place I assign to Providence in history, I will answer by saying that our God is the God of human hearts. I can truthfully say that I know, touch and adore His presence in human hearts. (May He be blessed for this grace that I have so often abused!) But history is written by men and the passions of men. I consider it the sum total, the frightful sum total of all our greeds since the murder of Abel. *Libido sciendi, libido sentiendi, libido dominandi,* these are the three rivers of fire that feed this history which builds up and knocks down civilizations, one after the other, one upon the other, into the same nothingness. Nevertheless man goes on. If this "inextricable depth of history," of which you spoke at Pleyel Hall, destroys all flesh, then, again to use your own words, it can do nothing against "the unique quality of man"—to be exact, the soul (why not name it?)—the soul which is governed, dominated, enslaved or in revolt, but always dependent on uncreated Love. It is, and it shall be forever. Heaven and earth may pass away, but you and I shall not pass.

Having thus fully outlined my Christian position, I again take my stand with my feet in the clay, even in the mud. If God does not manifest Himself in politics save by the terrible fruits of His absence (God's justice with regards to nations is always, it seems to me, negative), then we should operate in view of this absence without following in Machiavelli's footsteps, in accordance with nature, and carefully avoiding all the traps he laid. That is the problem we have to solve in our struggle against war. We indeed have to give in to this force of gravity that Simone Weil opposes to Grace, since this force is the law of politics, but we should try to direct it and choose the point at which we will fall, entrusting ourselves to the light of natural reason. We fight a war not with the language of sentiment, which is unintelligible to empires and those who govern them, but by using a tongue which they understand. We can win this game the stake of which is peace, if we offer in opposition to the current policy another which is more effective. What policy may that be?

Certainly not the one followed by the United States up to this month of December 1948. I have no reason to conceal from you my feelings about that. I should not like to write anything that might offend our American allies, but in the final analysis, one must confess that in politics they have shown a lack of imagination that verges on the criminal. In China, in Korea, in Greece, in fact wherever they have intervened, they have achieved the unbelievable result of making Stalin the beneficiary of offended national feelings and of the hatred which privileged classes arouse in all parts of the world when they have recourse to foreign aid in order to perpetuate themselves in power. No relief from this policy could come from a Britain still subject to the old Imperatives of the Commonwealth, and now more than ever incapable of that disinterested outlook which France, through all sorts of trials, and in spite of her poverty and disgrace, has kept fixed upon the outside world.

There should be for this France, once she gets out of the morass in which her parliamentarians have condemned her to vegetate, a policy of rebuilding the peace, not up in the clouds, or with unattainable ends as the goal, or suspended on utopias such as the United States of the World and other fiddle-faddle, but based on what is and cannot fail to be, namely, realities; and first and foremost, this reality: that Soviet Russia at the present time is not interested in war. She fears it. She would risk it only if an internal crisis—always awaited, always hoped for—were to put the adversary at her mercy,—a crisis, my dear Camus, of which one of the causes might very well be an uncontrolled movement started by some little man. That is the solid rock on which we could begin building. But here we run into the first obstacle, which is the impossibility of honest discussion between Soviet Russia and the West. This is definitely not a spiritual impossibility, because the Iron Curtain is most physical in nature. The Soviets have no greater concern than that of preserving their people from all liberal contamination. As this is for them a matter of life and death, and we must admit that from their point of view they are right (the contacts to which the war exposed the Red Army cost them dear), we would have to recognize this need and agree with the Kremlin that peace between the East and the West should be arrived at through intermediaries. France first of all, but not France alone. On the Russian side it would also be necessary to find representatives and intermediaries. Czechoslovakia from time to time has seemed disposed to play this role, if the Soviets were to consent to it. In the interview between Truman and Stalin that I visualize, the first pledge of good will would be to obtain from the Soviets a relaxing of the Iron Curtain and the promotion of some one of the satellite nations not certainly to the role of arbiter, but, to take an old word from the vocabulary of love and endearment, to that of go-between.

Taking this view, I would have no reason for rallying the R.P.F., as you thought I would. There is not a single one of the fatalities with which you seek to overwhelm me that I cannot surmount. I believe the R.P.F., no matter what happens, has no real influence on that section of the French people that has taken up Communism. It is because I have been a Gaullist from the very outset that I remain deeply attached to General de Gaulle. It is because I withdraw no part of the admiration and affection I have always had for André Malraux that I consider the idea of this Assemblage a bad one, and that I view its apparent success as an even sadder occurrence for these two destinies that have a place in my heart. General de Gaulle, by virtue of the independence he has always shown toward the Anglo-Saxons, could have been the one man designed above all others to find new roads in the direction of peace. I grant you that he would have had to overcome other tendencies of his nature, but that is not the topic we are discussing.

These views about peace that I offer you are only to be taken as suggestions. I leave it to the specialists to decide between them and others. But I do insist that an effective defense of peace is possible on the level of reason, even when we take into account this irrepressible instinct for power that drives the most liberal democracies, like Holland in Indonesia, or, at the present moment, Britain in Palestine, to refuse to yield a single inch, to run all risks, to gamble with the fate of mankind if necessary, rather than loosen their hold on a desert whose possession controls the defenses of their empire. Of what use is it to close our eyes? We shall never be able to suppress these antagonistic forces; but for a time perhaps we may succeed in equalizing them, as has already happened in the course of history. Have no fear: I am not going to give you a lecture on diplomatic history, and I am not a former student of the political sciences. However, these sciences exist. They have brought results. M. de Norpois promised the world periods of respite which would have been longer if M. de Norpois had been less bound by routine. However foolish he may have been, he does not seem to me as dangerous as some intellectuals who would entrust the saving of the world's peace to movements of an emotional origin, whose impulse they cannot direct and whose end they cannot foresee.

I understand that you people refuse to consider yourselves pacifists in the old sense of the word, that you have constructive ideas for a world parliament, that Garry Davis, by the attention he drew as soon as he appeared on the scene, has given evidence that the hour is now at hand to take a chance on it. For a long time now we have been watching the Big Wheel, a vestige of 1900, grinding the clouds in the sky above the Champ de Mars. I cannot become interested in these wheels that mesh on nothing, particularly the one you dream of constructing, which will have to undergo, even before it is finished, innumerable pressures of conflicting interests, as well as the relentless opposition of nations to anything that tries to limit their sovereignty.

Does this mean that there is nothing about your endeavor that I like? On the contrary, what I like about it is the very thing that I should like to create and preserve on other planes. You create new grounds for getting together, new possibilities of discussion and agreement among people who do not know one another. That follows the trend of my own thought, because you must not for an instant imagine that I renounce the use of spiritual weapons in the defense of peace. In my narrow sphere as a Christian layman, I am forced to utter this "cry repeated by a thousand sentinels," this "call of the hunters lost in the deep woods."

Travellers on earth that we are, we are separated by the abyss of generations, localities and classes. I, who travel alone, have the certainty of belonging to that small number who hold a lamp in the depth of the shadows, who in their unworthy hands have safeguarded the light they received in childhood, a light whose reflection I feel on my face and in my heart like those fiery figures of Georges de Latour. . . . Ah! Here I strike the chief obstacle that prevents me from attaching any importance to Garry Davis: there is a lack of balance between what is at stake and these campaigns in the press and the debating halls. The smoke from the crematories of Auschwitz, as it clears away, has shown us a humanity which now knows itself for what it is. The unclean policies of the surviving nations, even before they have finished the task of covering up these charnel houses, have the effect of making us realize by this evidence that the cause of mankind would indeed be desperate if there had not been the Incarnation, and if the Son of Man were not to return. The frightful simplification of history to which we are witnesses leaves no room for any illusions about our species, or about the fruits of death that it will continue to reap until its final total disintegration. We no longer have the right to hope that any human gesture is still possible that does not lead in the direction of death. Saint Cyran speaks somewhere of what stains every soul and "defames it before God." What has been defaming mankind before God since Auschwitz and Buchenwald (not to mention others, because what nation is not stained with crimes?) has surpassed all limits. We no longer have the right to hope that we will be able, just by ourselves, to save the peace of the world.

Above all, don't think that I presume to forbid Christians to take part in human endeavors. What I tell you applies only to me. All I have left is attention to a word, trust in a promise. I do not wish to let go of this fragment of a cloak that I cling to in the shadows, not even for a minute. But that concerns me alone. I open to you the thoughts of one who is on the wane; I speak to you as a man whose eyelids are becoming heavy, and who knows on what shoulder he hopes to be granted the grace of falling asleep.

IV

TO A LADY WHO WANTED TO SEND ME "THE DICTIONARY OF WEATHERVANES"

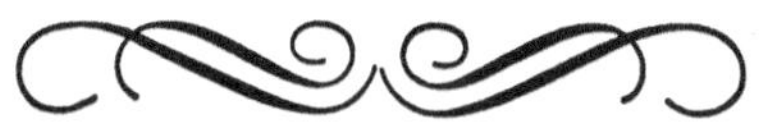

Believe me, Madame, you must give up this idea of offering me a copy of the Dictionary of Weathervanes, in which you say I have been given a prominent place. I thank you for your good intentions, but I would beg you to spare yourself this expense, because I confess that I do not entertain a very flattering opinion of the author. If he puts people in his dictionary for the purpose of maligning them, and if he holds that a change of opinion is the mark of a poor mind, I fear he is nothing but a fool, and what would I want with a book written by a fool? So far as I am concerned, I should not be proud to belong to that species of men whose ways of thinking were set in their youth, and who react at sixty as they did at twenty, not indeed to the wind that happens to be blowing, but in accordance with an inner urge forever blocked and broken by the same obstacles.

Do not fear, however, that I am trying to gild the lily. I understand that only political weathervanes are of interest to our man and, I imagine, to yourself, and that in your eyes I am one. To be perfectly frank, the one most common way of remaining steadfast in one's opinions is to be held that way by party requirements. I believe you will concede that all these mules, both young and old, who are held between the same shafts, sweat in the same harness, and make the same little Marxist or Maurrasian bells tinkle until they die deserve neither praise nor blame in this matter that concerns us. Everything depends upon the freedom of mind they have kept in spite of brace and bit. There are some who trot along meekly, and these, we know, are incapable of making a break: Claude Morgan, for instance. . . . But look at the foam and the streak of blood in the nostrils of Aragon! Oh, I do not mean to be malicious; I, too, have chafed at times under the harness. During the half century I have spent between the shafts, the various coachmen who have in turn occupied the driver's seat have watched me with an eye that was both affectionate and distrustful. Are they any surer of the old horse of today than they were of the untried young colt of former years? I wouldn't care to swear to it.

This, Madame, is the point I am trying to make: there is a kind of loyalty, on which I pride myself, that has always made me unwilling to bow to the directives of any party and that even in the Church (which with all my heart I wish to serve, and which I believe I have served well in my own way) has kept me from being one of its ever accommodating servants: this is the loyalty that arises from the determination to refuse to write anything that I do not truly believe. As a summation of my public life, I might very well deserve the one which the most illustrious son of my native Guyenne applied to himself: "Applauded on the right, applauded on the left, a Guelf to the Ghibellines, a Ghibelline to the Guelfs."

Come to think of it, isn't it strange that it is precisely this irreducible part of ourselves, which politics can never corrupt, that causes us to be numbered among the weathervanes? Any journalist would have been nothing but a weathervane if what he had written in July of 1940 about the victor of Verdun he had also written three months later about the treaty-maker of Montoire. In like manner, suppose that after collaborating in the clandestine *Lettres françaises* and the *Editions de minuit* with the Communists of the national front, I had managed, six months after the liberation, to remain faithful to this alliance and join the communizing third order, which would have meant serving, in the name of Stalin, the same gluttonous police-state monster that we had fought under Hitler. To give another example, I do not know whether or not André Gide is listed in the Dictionary of Weathervanes: keeping faith with himself, he publicly bore witness to the admiration he felt for the Communists, until the day came when this same loyalty to his own ideals prevented him from approving those things in the USSR which to him seemed worthy of condemnation. In his case, you will admit that rather than recant he might have yielded to the fear of being called a weathervane and pretended to admire things which from that point on only aroused his horror.

It is bad taste to praise oneself, and I am going to stop praising myself. It will perhaps surprise you if I confess that I am not very proud of this immobility and steadfastness in my principles which has almost invariably been the cause of fluctuations for which I have been reproached on the political plane. It will also surprise you that I seriously question myself on this score. We, who attach such great value to intellectual honesty, and who have suffered so much from the sins of conformity which certain leaders of thought have committed against it, have we ourselves always questioned what was not altogether clear to us? Have we not been satisfied with formulas given to us from the outside? Set your mind at ease: I am not aiming at those things which have to do with religion, because faith, and I mean living faith, is truly the least set and unchanging of all things, even when it is not a continuous staircase that follows the footsteps of saints; our relations with God (mine at any rate) are of an emotional nature and are stirred by the beating of the heart, just as any other sort of love is stirred. If in that respect I have marked time or stepped backwards, at least I have not stood still; or if I have, it has been with the false immobility of one who is bogged down. A Christian is delivered up not to the wild beasts, but to his own "deep mud," to quote the Scriptures—that mud from which the sinner must unceasingly try to extricate himself.

However, moved by this inner debate, I should like to make sure that I have not given to any other sort of question the same answer that was given me in my college days. If I react to certain problems, particularly those of a social nature, like the adolescent I was then, it is perhaps a sign that I have given them too little attention. You see, Madame, the point I am making; it is not my fluctuations that scandalize me, but rather the state of suspended judgment and watchful waiting which I thought was temporary, but which I find I still hold, and from which I feel I shall never depart. "To lend oneself to life's perfecting process . . ." Have I followed this advice that Barrès gave me when we parted? That is what really matters, not a servile, literal adherence to set rules. We feel indeed that a Maritain or a Gide, to take two types that are the antithesis of each other, have each developed in their own way according to inner models they had shaped for themselves. It matters little that Maritain has passed from Bergsonism to Thomism, that he underwent for a time the influence of Maurras only to turn violently against him later on; it matters still less that Gide was a Protestant, then the immoralist we know, or that he had periods of returning to Christianity, then this abrupt and passing taste for Communism. Through so many contradictory movements and eddies, these two lives have built themselves in accordance with their own inner laws, even the one of the two who chose what to us Christians is the evil way. Do you understand, Madame, that the life of every man worthy of the name ought to be at one and the same time a quest and a struggle, not a submission to political regulations and ideologies? How many minds does a Marx, a Nietzsche or a Maurras chain to his chariot! And how much security some people find in their chains! The real, basic question is not whether we have been weathervanes, but whether through the fear of seeming to be such we have let ourselves become prisoners of a system. "Axiom, religion, or prince of men?" wondered young Barrès in days gone by. Mollusk minds, like the hermit crab, seek from the outset a shell in which to hide. And even from the true faith, which should be life and soul to them, they draw only excuses for asking themselves no more questions about anything.

The marble of olden times chains us up to the loins

And every energetic man is like a god of boundaries.

Deceptive energy of confined men who work out their own confinement! Rather than a Dictionary of Weathervanes I should suggest to you, Madame, a dictionary of boundary gods, men set, fastened, congealed, petrified to the letter of the law, but from whom there arises from time to time, if they are poets, the mournful, musical plaint that the rising sun used to strike from the statue of Memnon.

I am letting my pen run along as if it were not to you that I am writing, as if there were any place in your pretty little head for reflections of this nature. To tell the truth, I am not very sure that you exist. But a man is ashamed to be caught openly talking to himself. We always talk to ourselves, yet nothing makes us look more insane than these soliloquies. Molière's valet talked to his cap, and I talk to you, Madame, so that I will not seem to be demented.

V

CONCERNING A CRIME AGAINST "CARMEN"

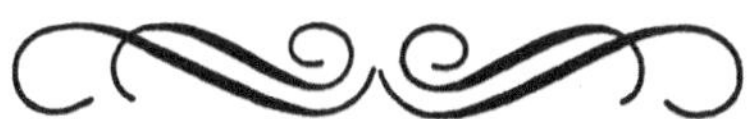

Dear Armande,

You are a woman of good taste. One might even say that taste is your specialty. I find you have no equal when it comes to judging things of the intellect and the amusements of the theatre. It is true that time, which ravages and destroys bodily beauty (though not that of a face as well molded as yours) confers upon a creature so endowed a sort of infallibility. Since you have gotten through the critical years, you have acquired a tone of assurance which is either amusing or irritating, according to the mood one is in. On any subject other than music, dancing, decorating and imaginative literature, you pretend you have nothing to say. As soon as the discussion touches upon politics, it is wonderful to watch your lovely gaze (one of the brightest I have ever admired in a woman) suddenly lose all expression. All at once, you resemble an allegory of absence. You vanish into the skies, from which you descend only if there suddenly resounds one of those fascinating first names like Bébé, Jean, Jeannot, Jean-Louis. Then from your little paper cloud, majestically, and holding in your little dimpled hand the scales of taste, which were adjusted once and for all by Christian Bérard, you give out your oracles. I am inclined to submit to this, dear Armande, just like any other mortal. Myself, I am not a man of taste; in fact, I am even less a man of taste than I seem to be. My secret judgments, were they made public, would lend weight to the opinion that Francis James once voiced about me: "Mauriac is a peasant. He is the peasant type. . . ." He thought he was scoffing, but he was really telling the truth without knowing it. I carefully disguise my peasant nature, and until lately I have left decisions about matters of taste to such celebrated specialists as yourself.

But all that has changed since a certain evening when your taste ran into my distaste with such violence that I really feel I must finally throw off my mask and deliver myself at one stroke of all the horror and contempt that certain inventions of your friends arouse in me. You delight in the company of a race of flies who can lay their eggs only in the heart of a masterpiece. They empty themselves on masterpieces, and that is the truth.

Of course it is more difficult to compose dance tunes than to make use of "Carmen" the way M. Roland Petit did! On the night of that sacrilegious ballet, in the lobby where you were parading a rapture that had the strength of law, you gave me to understand that it was fortunate that old masterpieces might still serve for something like that. I must confess that in that opinion you had the support of an audience from the big night clubs and grand premières, who cried "Author! Author!", as if one could put the name of an author on filthy finger-marks sullying a sublime poem. The author actually appeared, before a stamping roomful of people. How happy I should have been if I could have directed with sure aim one powerful spray of Flit on this little, black, highly acclaimed man! Back of me I heard the grumbling voice of an old gentleman who shared my feelings of anger and contempt; it was M. Jacques Rouché. I was also consoled to see my own suffering reflected on the astounded faces of Sauguet, d'Auric and Jacques Février.

This matter is serious, and goes far, far beyond our disagreement about a seasonal ballet which is now far in the past. What the sneering of your friends before masterpieces betokens is that there is a certain kind of taste which is the enemy of all that is beautiful. It is a sly enemy, which does not attack frontally, but messes, deforms and dirties. The last act of "Carmen," that ascending movement of love toward death, that old, commonplace story of the human couple, that eternal "You don't love me any more!"—"No, I don't love you any more!"—what contempt they really have for it! How perfectly it is all presented to us as an object of laughter! Once in a while, a whiff of "Carmen" detached itself from this obscene pantomime and was wafted in our direction, like a breath of fresh sea air full of salt and iodine, suddenly stronger than the odor of this field of manure at our feet.

There is no doubt that you have the right to pitch your tent in this realm of the kind of taste whose boundaries have been set by our dear Bérard, and in which ballet masters, stage designers, decorators, worldly aesthetes and two or three famous dressmakers hold the post of augurs. The replacement of a masterpiece by a setting is an unwritten law with this little world that hates nature in all its forms. That is their first law. But there is another law which is more secret. I recall the title of a forgotten work of Barrès: "Any license except against love." For his deficiencies and vices, man is accountable only to God. Perhaps there is no one who does not have, like

Saint Paul, a thorn in his flesh, or an imp of Satan attached to his footsteps, slapping him on. But the artist has a special obligation: that of breaking clear, at all costs, from the black circle drawn around his inspiration by the black angel. Those you admire, on the contrary, craftily seek to draw everything inside this accursed circle. Not satisfied to be its prisoners, they aspire to lock in the rest of the world with them, and they drag in, to dishonor them, the heroes of simple and pure masterpieces. Let them leave Don José weeping on his knees over the stabbed body of Carmen; this story does not concern them. These words of Pascal come to my mind: "They blaspheme that of which they are ignorant." They might at least remember. Are you so filled with poisons that you no longer recognize in the music of the masters the hopes and dreams with which your own youth had filled it? When you scoff at that music, are you not really scoffing at the tender memories of your own youth?

You will reply, dear Armande, that after all it was nothing but an entertainment, and that I am making much ado about nothing. About nothing: one could not pick a better phrase, unless dregs and scum are something. But since that fatal evening I have had this nothing on my heart. Now I feel wonderfully relieved.

VI

TO A "ROUND TABLE" SUBSCRIBER

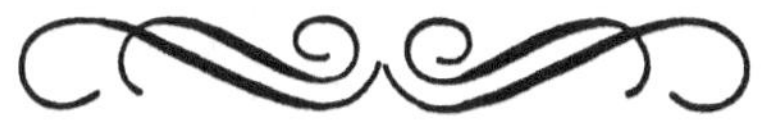

Dear Subscriber,

I do not claim to speak in the name of the "Round Table"; we are not a school, and there are no masters or disciples among us. But after eighteen months of existence our review has come to a turning-point, and I have to ask myself this question: "Does it have a reason for its existence? Does it fill a need?" I should like to make a genuine effort at offering a clear statement as to its "general policy" as I see it. But do we really have one?

When we began putting out the "Round Table," our plan was not over-ambitious. We were not aiming to change the world. What were we actually trying to do? First, to provide, on a modest scale, what seemed to be lacking elsewhere; second, to rally to our banners all French writers worthy of the name whom the sinister events of our more recent history had torn apart. It seems to me that up to a certain point we have succeeded, and without stirring up too much controversy. The few wolves who howled were not themselves too convinced. They felt, as we do, that the spirit breathes where it wishes, that Vercors does not suffice for everything, that no one has the right to impoverish the French literary heritage, or to deprive it of the names and works that are its glory. None of us has disowned what at one time he believed to be true. We have forced no one to proclaim his errors. The fact that some names appear together in our table of contents does not carry over into life, nor does it mean that in political or ideological matters yesterday's adversaries are reconciled; but none of those who write for us considers himself so perfect that he cannot permit his name to appear on the review's cover along with the names of other writers of whose conduct he has only recently had occasion to disapprove.

Thus the "Round Table," in a France more divided than it ever was before, offers to minds of good faith a common meeting ground where, by mutual agreement, each one lays down his arms, or at least those of his arms which are poisoned by political hatred. We again create the possibility of exchange of thought and discussion. Shall we succeed in rebuilding a compass such as "La Nouvelle Revue Française" was up until 1940, where the qualified representatives of all literary generations voiced their thoughts? Of that we are not too sure. The France of 1949 is not only divided against itself, since the great catastrophe of the enemy occupation; the different philosophies, like the different political parties, today have mouthpieces that are filled with arrogance. Each one claims to officiate on his own account and wants to set up his own little church; I mean his own personal review. At the outset, we had hoped to have a meeting of three generations. Malraux and Camus were to have been the chosen delegates for the people of their age. At first they seemed to go along with the idea, but soon we had to accept disillusionment. We shed a tear when, after the second issue, Sisyphe fled our company and went off to roll his own little personal stone all by himself. Then we realized something: a review is shaped and takes its true form thanks to those who leave it or are afraid of it. At first we approached most of the young "important" members of the press; but from the very first contact, before they even opened their mouths, I realized that our sublime ones would have nothing to do with it. On the other hand, some of the better writers of their generation were to seek us out of their own accord and give the "Round Table" some of its directives; and they were the very ones we had not even thought of.

What did they find in the "Round Table"? First of

all, a shelter from professional philosophers and a secure place where the meaning of language would not be brought up for discussion. That, it seems to me, is important. I believe that the sterility of imaginative literature in present-day France stems from the fact that for many people language has lost its value as an instrument and tool, and the word has become an end to itself. We do not at all underestimate the interest of the research of people like Maurice Blanchot; we merely believe that it is rendering literature a service to offer young writers a chance to collaborate in a review where the question of semantics will not be brought up.

We definitely believe that true style is achieved by not having any, and that in the best writers its invisibility gives proof of its existence. But some bob-tailed foxes, not being themselves writers, have tried to convince young Frenchmen that style is no longer in style. We, however, are simple people. We have a tendency (perhaps a guilty one, if we are Christians) to accept the idea advanced by Gide many years ago, in the preface to his *L'Immoraliste*: "In art there is no problem for which the work of art itself is not a sufficient solution." The Gide of 1902 further wrote: "Besides, I have sought to prove nothing, but only to paint well and throw the proper light on my painting." In truth, both God and the devil know that with *L'Immoraliste* he had tried to prove something. But to paint well, to light one's painting well! There is no better opening rule of the game that one can offer young writers so that they may escape from this terror that haunts the realms of literature. Let them not believe those who preach that literature has no other reason for being except its enlistment in the service of revolutionary syndicalism, emancipation of the blacks, sex education, and things of that nature! Of course it has a mission "in the centuries and in the heavens," which is to bear witness to mankind:

Because it is truly, Lord, the best testimonial
That we can give our dignity. . . .

And this testimonial should be impartial and free. To any born artist, this admits of no discussion. You who try to enlist us give yourselves away as strangers to the family.

Neither do we believe in a set formula from which one dare not deviate when he writes a novel. This crisis of the French novel that is drummed in our ears will be solved on the day when young French writers manage to rid themselves of the idea that Joyce, Kafka and Faulkner hold the Tables of the Law which determine the technique of the novel. There is a whole catechism dealing with the way one must introduce the weather in a novel, the rights and duties of the novelist with regard to his characters, the liberties he must allow them, and what he is supposed to know and not to know about them. A whole generation of writers has had to undergo the sterilizing effects of this arbitrary protocol imposed by philosophers who have "stolen the tool."

The truth is that each novelist must devise his own technique. Every novel worthy of the name constitutes a planet, large or small, which secretes its own special laws just as it produces its own flora and fauna. Faulkner's technique is without doubt the best possible technique with which to paint a Faulknerian universe. Kafka's nightmare has created the myth that makes it contagious. Benjamin Constant, Stendhal, Eugene Fromentin, Jacques Rivière, Radiguet have used other techniques, taken other liberties, erected other hurdles for themselves. But for the technical problem, as for all others, the work of art, whether it be called *Adolphe, Lucien Leuwen, Dominique* or *Diable au corps* or *À la Recherche du temps perdu,* is still a sufficient solution.

Let no one get the idea that we are particularly hostile to philosophy. But we should like to be philosophers without knowing it, philosophers who carry no banner. Montaigne and Pascal and all our sermonisers and moralists have shown us that one can go very far in the knowledge of man by using the language of simple people. We should like for people to be able to read our review without having to consult Lalande's vocabulary. In this respect, I believe the "Round Table" has a special mission: to approach all subjects, even the most difficult, to make obscure things intelligible without jargonizing, without betraying the language of which we are the heirs and guardians, and by its mere presence to prove to other reviews that they are technical and specialized.

The spectres of madmen handled like puppets in the vicinity of Saint-Germain-des-Prés by second-generation pseudo-surrealists do not impress us to the point where we have to fall back on old formulas and subscribe to the forms of a dead past. We were born, we live, we move about in an atmosphere that Freud, Proust, Surrealism and the Existentialist philosophers have been altering since the time of our youth. Whether it has been enriched or poisoned thereby, certainly living authors cannot avoid breathing it. For them, it is not a question of systematically denying or rejecting anything. What they reject are the words of authority, the prohibitions, the things they have not assimilated, the things that have not turned to flesh and blood within them.

The physical sensation of an imposture that we feel before a canvas of Dubuffet, or when listening to the inarticulate cries that madness drew from poor Artaud, while critics gravely made notes and wrote commentaries about them, is what made us distrust poetry and kept us from publishing poems. At our first editorial meeting I suggested that we inscribe on the cover of the review: "Note: poets are requested not to contribute." It was only my love of poetry that inspired this quip. The truth is that there is no one left today who could render a valid judgment in the field of poetry. All the muses are at Sainte-Anne, howling behind the bars. Words, abandoned to their own devices, group themselves at random, and an obscure muttering covers the eternal song. We have achieved that season predicted by Rimbaud: "And the springtime brought me the frightful laughter of the idiot." We shall have to wait until this laughter wears itself out and dies away. What is poetry? I know of no definition that satisfies me better than that of Thierry Maulnier: "The true mission of poetry is to offer to the best there is in language and to the most mysterious that there is in the world a place where the two can miraculously meet."

The best there is in language has for us a precise meaning. When, as and if we shall publish a poem, we shall know the reasons for our choice, and we shall be able to set them forth. "We." Who is this "we"? When I started this letter, I claimed that I was not speaking for anyone. I must restate that in concluding. My pen ran away with me when I wrote "we." These pages perhaps attest my solitude, and are born from the need of holding round about me the remnants of a decomposed world.

However, the "Round Table" exists. It is a compendium that gathers the generations together and draws close the names of writers separated by history, where a whole youthful generation shows by living chronicles that it scoffs at the interdictions of pseudo-surrealism. It therefore suffices to convince us that we are forging a link in the chain broken by the disaster of 1940, and that on a modest scale we are again creating for French letters some of the conditions necessary for their permanence and continuity.

VII

CONCERNING THE CLAUDEL–GIDE CORRESPONDENCE

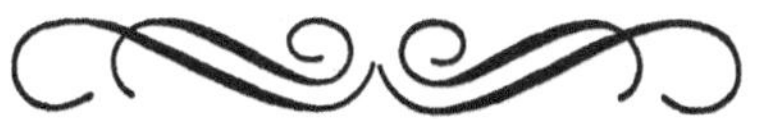

If we survive with God in the hereafter, dear Jacques Rivière, in substantially the same form we had on earth, I do not believe that you can remain indifferent to this correspondence between Gide and Claudel, which has been published by *Le Figaro littéraire* and which reveals the deepest secrets of at least one of these two lives. It has been holding my interest ever since I read it in a state of intense and rather gloomy reverie in which you played a part. If you had lived as long as I, perhaps you would have kept, as I have, the trust of an old child in elders whom he blindly admires and cherishes. From the depths of the gulf of light that surrounds you, I can imagine your look of sadness and reproach fixed upon these letters open to all, documents of a lawsuit pleaded and lost, which are no longer of interest save as literary history.

You remember what they meant to the boys we once were. Of course we had not read them, but we knew of their existence. This discussion between the poet of the *Grandes Odes* and the author of the *Nourritures terrestres* concerned each one of us in particular, because the matter under discussion went far beyond the oddities of *Corydon.* What Christian of twenty was not torn between two opposing temptations: that of the God of Claudel and His exacting love, and that of the delightful world where "everything is allowed"?

Consequently, there is about this correspondence a kind of desecration. It reminds one of old pieces of furniture made sacred to us by the contact of our dead and by childhood memories, now torn from the holy gloom of the sold house and waiting on the sidewalk, under an indifferent sun, for the hour of the auction. This sale before death, more than any event of international life, brings me face to face with the final evidence that we belong to a society in full process of liquidation.

I shall get over my anguish. I should be tempted to write that with your help I shall try to draw from these letters a lesson that concerns only us two, provided I had the privilege of troubling your ineffable peace with my disasters, dear Jacques. These pathetic letters force me to reflect on the condition of a strange animal, the man of letters, and on this law of the species to which I still belong and which was yours as well, the law that bids us not to leave this world without telling everything about ourselves and without taking away with us the certainty that the files we leave behind are complete, that no part of them has been overlooked, even if our memory should suffer terribly in consequence.

Since the days of Jean-Jacques and Chateaubriand, it is no longer the work that matters, but rather the drama of its author, which it comments upon and enhances by its imagery. Everything is done as if the author had no doubt that his mission is to assume for centuries to come a certain well-defined human type. The portrait must be complete, and from then on no one may add the slightest retouch.

In André Gide this foregone-conclusion attitude is curiously strengthened because it springs from ethics. The man who wrote *Corydon* and who chose to go forward in life with face bared, holding his mask in his hand, wanted our grand-nephews to be able to penetrate his personality beyond the shadow of a doubt. So he opens up to them the most secret documents, those journals in which a man who no longer prays sometimes relieves himself of the burden that he despairs of bearing all alone. It is as though he made a hole in the ground and buried his face in it while he poured into an unknown ear the unspeakable secret of his destiny. Thus we can understand Gide's consenting to the publication of his letters in the *Figaro littéraire*, even though we suffer from it. Perhaps from where you are, dear Jacques, you can understand it even better. This consent springs from an attitude that has been set for years.

Dare I say that I find it less easy to penetrate the reasons of Paul Claudel? Why did he agree to this publication? After all, Gide is still alive, his case is still before the courts, the last word concerning him has not been spoken. Am I wrong in viewing this sale of Claudel's letters to Gide as a premature renunciation? "The case is closed" he seems to say to us. Not at all. Our manuscripts are not collected until we die. You know that, Jacques, you who were saved at the last second, and whose final words were: "And now I know that I am miraculously saved." One would say that so far as Claudel is concerned, Gide is already judged, that we have to give up the game. I believe we can still persist on another plane, that of prayer and sacrifice. But this correspondence thrown open to the public by Claudel makes one think that in his eyes the bets have been made, and that he judges that henceforth such efforts as he formerly made in behalf of an exceptional soul are without object.

Why "exceptional"? Here we touch upon a doubt

that I myself feel and that perhaps Claudel has also experienced. Catholic writers have waged this battle for a soul that appeared to us precious above all others in the obscure belief that a great writer has greater value in the eyes of the Supreme Being than the humble Christian of the streets. We have made the error of transposing to an eternal plane the prestige that an admirable artist enjoyed in our eyes. The Church's total disdain for novels and other idle tales of literary people ought to prepare us for the rather humiliating mercy which will perhaps envelop all the literati on Judgment Day. On that day, I imagine, our books will not at all be taken into account, either to crush us with blame or to heap merit upon us; they will simply not exist in the thought of this God Who knows and understands the inmost secrets of the human heart, and Who has no need of these testimonies we heap upon ourselves, or these retouched portraits of ourselves in which we strike a pose—in short, our books.

Perhaps Claudel, who is himself the author of that overwhelming epitome, "the man of letters, the assassin and the prostitute," realized that all the priests and all the faithful who pray and suffer in secret for the salvation of a great writer, though they would not do as much for the chestnut vendor on the corner, overrate immeasurably the importance of men of letters. We are in reality brothers to comedians, and still more to prostitutes, by reason of our comportment, which consists in losing our own personality, putting on that of others, giving ourselves to the first-comer, opening up our hearts as others do their bodies, and selling ourselves.

But perhaps Claudel, like André Gide, nurses the anxiety of adding a feature to the picture he will leave of himself. How strange that must seem to you where you are, dear Jacques! How can we fail to admire in these two great writers who are so greatly at odds with each other the same belief in that derisive eternity promised in the manuals of literature? Yet it is a faith that one is tempted to view as comic today, when all the witches, all the sybils, all the Cassandras warn us that our generation will have no posterity.

Is it perhaps because, despite this civilization which is crumbling around them, our old masters draw consolation from the thought that from Antigone to pious Aeneas practically all the heroes of the ancient world were able to clear a path to us across the debris of Athens, Carthage and Rome, and that on the still smoking ruins of Europe the Golden Ass of Apuleius continues to wiggle his obscene ears?

Thus we people of letters dream that beyond the atomic age the creatures we have invented will still have a place in the hearts and minds of the survivors. What folly! Yet we all partake of it, from Claudel to the most recent Goncourt prizewinner.

The believer and the atheist hope for the same fortune for their characters. The frail Gidian caravels and the stout ships of Claudel set sail with a passionate belief in this immortality in the memory of men which is only genuine nothingness. Even the believer does not refrain from hoping in this dust, these ashes, this nothingness.

As for our Gide, we, the living, can do nothing more for him. You alone, dear Jacques, may be able to speak to him during the hours of the night when he is sitting up and thinking. He will recognize your friendly voice. Say to him: "Dear Gide, this correspondence that you are handing over to every comer, this document to be used just like any other in telling your story, constitutes only an episode in a drama whose outcome is still unknown. It is an awkward and abortive effort, but its miscarriage gives us no authority to make any prejudgment concerning the final vicissitude—the only one that really matters. You have not had the Grace to be born in the bosom of Holy Mother Church, or to follow the royal highway she has blazed to Eternal Life; but there are goat-paths that lead to God, too."

Guide him, dear Jacques, to one of these hidden paths. Help him to cross alone the border beyond which reigns this Love in which you believed.

VIII

SCOUTS AND GUIDES

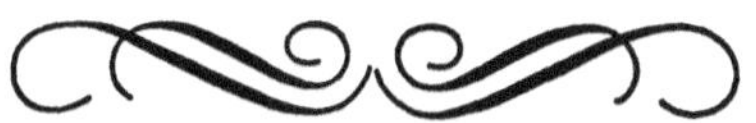

My dear Pierre Schaeffer,

Your novel *Les Enfants de coeur* affected me, but certainly not as a novel; nothing in it appeals to my imagination. I even doubt that a man who has grown up and lived outside the Catholic atmosphere, no matter how cultured, would be able to grasp what it's all about. When I first knew you, you were just leaving one of our larger schools, the 10th, if memory serves me. But you were, above everything else, a Scout; you were pursuing, under the name of *routier*, the dream that had its roots in your childhood. The *Route* was a childhood miracle pursued beyond adolescence. At twenty, you still wore your little boy's disguise. You led the same rondo around the same bonfire and the same cassock. You managed the team of the *Magian Kings*, and invented farces and mysteries for the edification of the fake peasants of the big suburb. In the *Magian Kings*, the spirit of the scouts and the spirit of the 10th formed a precipitate of odd taste which is well described by the remark you report from one of your comrades: "Just the same, the Lord is a remarkable fellow!"

Am I wrong in recognizing in the Father who stirred up this beautiful fire, and whom you call Father Diamant, the illustrious priest whose apostolic career, by a detour of Providence, has just wound up in Hollywood? We shall come back to that. What your book describes is a "flight itinerary." You don't definitely say so, but we see you from page to page tearing yourself away from the enchantment of prolonged childhood. You suddenly discover that you are an adult, and that life is there before you, not simple and tranquil, but harsh and criminal. Indeed, it seems that for you everything that the Church puts at the disposal of the faithful has been a party to this vanished enchantment. God keep me from suggesting that you have turned away from the Faith. It doesn't help matters any that along with your book I received another which seems to have become your Bible, and which you say you want to discuss with me, the *Fragments d'un enseignement inconnu.* Its author, P. D. Ouspensky, was the spiritual heir of that mysterious Gurdjeff who gathered together some fanatical followers at the Château of Prieuré, near Fontainebleau; it was there that Catherine Mansfield came to die, like a mortally wounded doe in the mud of a pool.

The almost physical aversion I feel for anything that closely or remotely resembles theosophy, the mistrust that the tenets of gnosis and esoteric Christianity arouse within me, would suffice to keep me from having any discussion with you about this "unknown instruction" without deep previous study. Besides, that is not my intention. In your case, the only thing that arouses my attention is that a young Catholic, subjected to certain methods of apostleship in vogue among young students, is led astray at the age of forty, lured by another wisdom. Once again, it matters little that this new wisdom does not bar any particular religion. Catholicism alone is no longer enough for you. That is the fact that concerns us both, because it opposes a defiance and a negation to the promise that a woman of Samaria, and through her all of us, received from the Lord at Jacob's Well: "Whosoever shall drink of this water shall still thirst, but he who drinks of the water I shall give him shall nevermore thirst."

You have drunk, and still you thirst, and lean your disillusioned face over another fountain. A story that has been repeated a thousand times, you will tell me. No indeed! Most of the people who fall away from Christianity have not lived it as you have; they give up something they never really had. You, on the contrary, whether you like or not, are the embodiment of a failure: the failure of a certain method? I realize that each case of this sort should be studied by itself, and that secrecy is required. Rest assured: I do not wish to discuss in public your private life, about which I know nothing. We do not need to know whether you have failed Grace, or whether Grace has failed you. I am merely searching for what there is that is artificial in the picture that your novel gives us of this little world of scouts and guides in which you grew up.

In one chapter of *Enfants de coeur*, you recall that one night, when I went camping with you, I rather displeased your comrades. I remember how they themselves cut me, who am completely impulsive and discipline my moods so little that people can say anything about me save that I am not natural. But what made their atmosphere so unbreathable to me was precisely their lack of naturalness, a behavior which seemed to me at all times to be mechanical. They were Catholic scouts, but they were also boys who wanted to be free and were straining at their leash. Your chaplain, who was at the same time comradely and a little aloof, watched me with a smile on the corner of his mouth, while keeping his distance. The certainty of belonging to the elite of elites (being from the 10th) was oddly blended in you with the fear of not being quite "up to snuff." The school spirit of the polytechnician, the team spirit of the guides, the practice of virtue and apostleship, kept alive in all of you a visible and quite understandable satisfaction. Yet I felt that you were full of distrust. You prowled gropingly around certain books. Literature seemed to you to be a possible meeting place with spirits of another race, with "the ends which are only the ends" of which Pascal speaks. But one was struck with the fact that you were not at your ease. Entangled in your complexes, you resembled guinea-pigs designed for spiritual experimenters like your famous Father Diamant.

God forbid, my dear Pierre Schaeffer, that I should pass judgment on this priest who has devoted the best part of his life to young people. I do not doubt that he has started a great many of them toward the light, which is enough to assure his glory in this world and the next. The fact remains, however, that you were being "prepared" for a certain experiment, which might succeed or miss fire, as the case might be. I recall a book of this Father (the story of a scout pilgrimage to Rome) where one sees him in the final pages seizing a boy around the waist and throwing him alive into the brazier of God. As I read this, I could not help conjuring up the bull of Phalaris. The visible delights of the sacrificing high priest, which every word betrayed, aroused in me an anxiety that has not been dispelled over the years.

This anxiety does not touch the fundamental truth. The Son of Man still continues to be for me the Son of God. It is the method that was applied to you that I question. Taken back to its basic foundation, the problem I place before myself is this: from the point of view of Faith, there exist from the outset, between Grace and each chosen soul, certain exchanges of which the soul is the only witness and the sole object. It is the "I and my Creator" of Newman. Things that come from the outside, like collective exercises and group rites, are supposed to aid what goes on within. But in what measure is the inner experience served, and to what extent is it perverted, by these activities? I realize that they have as their aim the reviving of sentiments that may no longer exist, that it is a matter of stirring up discussion between the creature and his Creator, of making the heart sensitive to God.

It is in this sense that Pascal invites us to bow to the automaton: "Because we must not fail to recognize ourselves," he writes, "We are as much automaton as mind." Here I rebel against Pascal. There comes a moment, and you are an example of it, when the mind finally exerts judgment over the automaton to which we have tied it. Scout automatism did not overcome your anguish. You challenged your religious life as soon as it seemed to you to be bound to a mechanism set in motion by specialists who knew how to manipulate it, and all the more so because they were dealing with a young quarry who had no defense or tricks.

We must therefore go back to the source, far beyond all induced fervors. We must hold fast to the unique authenticity of Faith, Faith in the shadows, the crucifying happiness that Christ announced to Thomas: "Blessed are those who have not seen and have believed" . . . who have not seen, have not heard, have not touched, have not been enlightened. Everything that is perceptible to the senses comes from the periphery and concerns it. What role does God play in what is externally induced? Least authentic, according to Pascal's story, are perhaps his tears of joy. What you have broken away from, dear Pierre Schaeffer, is not Christ, but a system of emotions aroused about Christ; in short, a technique. I admit that with some boys who are frustrated for satisfactions of the flesh, it may seem necessary to provide some appeasements which, in order to be spiritual, must appeal to the heart as well. I do not deny that they may sometimes come from God. But how can we be sure of it, since they are the result of a certain mode of life, of automatism? Perhaps in our declining years we are better prepared to understand, in man, the greatness of a love that expects from God no exchange perceptible to the senses and requires no answer. Indeed, at the moment when the old man realizes that in human love, if he still experiences it, there is nothing to expect, nothing to hope for, he also realizes that if he turns to God he retains his faith in the infinite Love of which he knows himself to be the object, even though nothing comes to him from that side that the senses can discern.

I fear that all we have in our religion that is of an effusive nature ought to be erased. Our greatness comes from this love of adoration which is aroused in us by the *Deus absconditus*, the hidden God, the inaccessible God, the God Who is imperceptible to the heart. At the boundary are the astonishing words of Dostoievsky in a letter written when he left prison, words which he was to put, twenty years later, into the mouth of one of his "Possessed": "If someone were to prove to me that Christ is without truth, and that it is true that truth is without Christ, then I should prefer to stay with Christ rather than with the truth." We know that no power on earth will be able to produce this proof, since Christ is truth. But we are determined in advance not to be separated from Christ by anything, no matter what; neither by His apparent absence, nor by His silence. We are determined to have recourse to no subterfuge that might lead us astray. It is the cry of Saint Paul, that the lowliest Christian has the right to take up again in the shadows of his faith without consolation: "Who shall separate us from the love of Christ? Will it be tribulation, or anguish, or persecution, or hunger, or nakedness, or peril, or the sword? But in all these trials we are more than conquerors, through the One Who has loved us. For I have the assurance that neither death, nor life, nor angels, nor kingdoms, nor things present, nor things to come, nor powers, nor height, nor depth, nor any other creature shall separate us from the love of God in Jesus Christ our Lord." And we might add: "Nor silence, nor night."

Dear Pierre Schaeffer, to the poor lark, once the mirror is broken, there is left only the sunshine of Christ, which our human eyes do not see, the sunshine of the shadows. And the poor lark continues to yield to the call of the first charmer to come along; still dangling from his foot Father Diamant's broken strings, it flutters around an initiating high-priest. But our story with Christ can admit of only two characters: Christ and each one of us; and between the two, of only one interpreter, the Church of Simon Peter, the Church of the laying on of hands, the holder of the master-words that bless and absolve.

These, my dear *enfant de coeur*, are the thoughts which the reading of your book inspired in the old *enfant de coeur* that I still am.

IX

MORE ABOUT SCOUTS AND GUIDES

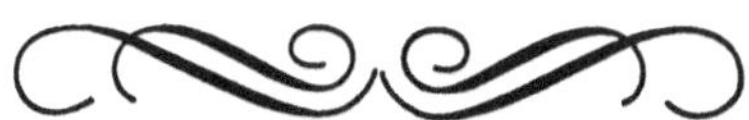

No, indeed, Sir, I do not dislike the Scout movement, and you have completely misunderstood the purport of my letter to Pierre Schaeffer. I am as fully convinced as you that generations of children and adolescents have greatly benefited from Scout methods. But we are not talking about them. Pierre Schaeffer's story calls our attention to Guides who are past the adolescent stage. Our common drama starts with that brief interval between springtime and summer when the adolescent turns into a man. How many times, since 1910, when Barrès quoted them in an article about my first verses, have I repeated to myself the words of Sainte-Beuve: "To ripen, to ripen, that is the problem; we harden in spots and spoil in others, but we don't ripen." These words are particularly applicable to over-sensitive boys marked with the sign of the poet who, if they are Christians, are predisposed to seek in religion those pious delights which are always suspect.

It would be easy to show that nearly all of us

have been, as Claudel says of Rimbaud, "a child badly transformed into a man." The difficulty of being is really the difficulty of becoming. Barrès handed me this rebuff at the dawn of my career, when he wrote about *Mains jointes*: "We must walk away from our youth with a firm step, and find something better. It is not so wonderful to be a wonder at twenty. What is difficult is to adapt oneself to life's molding hand, and to draw enrichment out of life even as it snatches its first gifts away from us." May one say that the Guides do not surmount the difficulty of being, but merely by-pass it? This viewpoint still seems too narrow to me. My letter which shocked you dealt with a far more serious matter.

What is involved in this debate is the method used by the Churches in connection with masculine youth. You are quite wrong in suspecting me of trying to pick a quarrel with the illustrious Jesuit whom Pierre Schaeffer in his story calls Father Diamant. If it is true, as some of his former disciples assure me, that this Father, having discovered at the age of forty *Les Nourritures terrestres*, believed that the fervor inspired by Gide in his Nathanael could be transposed and in some way channeled toward Heaven, we would have a good chance of denouncing his imprudence and proving that he was the dupe of an over-seductive demon (and which one of us has this demon not seduced? But then we are not Jesuits!). That would still be restricting the import of my letter. The entire debate that it raises is contained in this sentence which you will forgive me for repeating: "From the point of view of faith, there exist from the outset, between Grace and each chosen soul, certain exchanges of which the soul is the only witness and the sole object. It is the 'I and my Creator' of Newman. Things that come from the outside, like collective exercises and group rites, are supposed to aid what goes on within. But in what measure is the inner experience served, and to what extent is it perverted, by these activities?"

If I come back to this question which I have already raised, it is because today I should like to give it an answer whispered into my ear by a dead man during the time that has since elapsed. The man is Emmanuel Mounier, who seems closer to us than ever now that he is no longer here, at least to those of us who were not his personal friends and who, having had with him only spiritual contacts, have not yet felt his absence; but actually he was never more present than in this total picture that death has given of him.

Emmanuel Mounier, it seems, never tried to convert anyone; he had no direct method for gathering young minds into the Church's nets or for holding them there. I do not know whether in the *Esprit* groups the believers and "practicers" were in the majority. Perhaps Mounier himself never tried to find out. He simply lived his Christian life among his fellow-men. The only thing that concerned him was to help them find, here and now, an answer to the questions of every sort that they raised. The lamp that he held high over his generation and with which he cleared up every problem was that of the Gospel. He advanced in this light, but as though it were of value only to him. To him, it would have seemed a silly idea to treat his comrades like some sort of spiritual quarry, or to keep, as did one converter I knew, a memorandum book of the chase, with a listing of the heads of game taken. He worked among them and for them without trying to make any impression on their consciousness save by the example of his own life; in short, his was the same apostleship, but on an intellectual level, as that of the worker-priest in the factory; and it was not an accident that it was one of them who prayed over his remains. Emmanuel Mounier was a member of a team. He showed the others of the team by his comportment what the fruits of an authentic Christian life are. The rest was up to Grace. He had no pretension of arousing it or of offering himself as a substitute for it.

The words so often repeated by Léon Bloy that "the only misfortune is not to be a saint" now take on a particular meaning. If there really is no worse misfortune, it is because on the spiritual level no other force but saintliness has any effect by its mere presence. The conquests of saintliness are not of the same kind as those achieved by means of a technique elaborated and brought to perfection by pious specialists. Catholic writers of the generations that preceded Mounier, or at least many among them, did not understand, or understood too late, that to be redeemed by Christ they first had to conform to Christ, not to celebrate Him in prose and verse. It is the living Christ in a man that converts other men; one must see Him in order to believe in Him.

I don't condemn or even disapprove of the drill-ground techniques that serve to make up the bulk of the army. But the creation of an elite calls for different methods. Christianity cannot be an embellishment, an orchestration of life, a fairyland. Like a trusting child asleep in the woods, Pierre Schaeffer awakens after a long sleep; he is dressed like a little boy. He looks at his short pants. In his dream he was playing cowboys and Indians, but he is forty years old. While he slept, millions of men tortured and slew millions of other men. Half the planet is in the hands of Christ's mortal enemies, the other half in the hands of the camouflaged enemies of Christ and His Church. A world is in the ascendant for which Christ refused to pray, the world of power and pleasure and the crushing of the poor beneath the weight of gold. While Pierre Schaeffer slept, the annihilation of the human being by Soviet "genetics" and of the planet by atomic weapons have become current topics in all of the world's newspapers.

To sum it up, we who are Christians must give the answer, but not with lyrics or blank verse. Our life itself must be our answer, a life lived in the very midst of these people subjected to so many formidable ferments. For men of my age, the game is over; our copy has been handed in. But you young people have a choice to make, and no one can do it for you. A Father Depierre in his factory, an Emmanuel Mounier in *Esprit* have embraced the grief of mankind, each according to his calling. But first they have renounced everything else in order to consummate these nuptials. One of my books is entitled "God *and* Mammon"; it is not entitled "God *or* Mammon." The conjunction is the significant word, the one that marks in the destiny of a human being the victory of God or His defeat.

I fear, Sir, that my reply disappoints you. Indeed, how could it fail to do so? Through you, I am replying to myself. Through the *Routiers*, I am striking out at myself, because I amused myself with fires far less innocent than the campfires and other bucolic pieties from which you have not yet turned away. Old age is a time when one no longer talks to anyone but himself, even though he pretends to be talking to others.

X

TO JEAN COCTEAU, ON THE SUBJECT OF *BACCHUS*

Don't believe everything you read in the papers, my dear Cocteau. I was not furious when I left Marigny the other evening. I was not raging. I was simply sad because a whole roomful of people, all of Paris crowded together, had been able to listen without a cry of protest to that comedian disguised as a bishop who used the words of the Lord's Prayer to get a laugh: the Lord's Prayer which, to quote an abbess of Solesmes, is "that unique prayer that the Church puts on the lips of the priest when, in the very heart of the cloud, he stands face to face with God in the midst of the sacred mysteries." I felt sorry for all of us, and most of all for you. Don't worry; I am not writing this to hurt you. It would be so easy to hurt you! Too easy. For forty years we have been members of a troupe in the same circus, both in the wings and in the ring, so how could we fail to know each other's strong and weak points? I have been watching you do your act for nearly half a century. You have more than one trick in your bag, but I know them all. You are at the same time the toughest and the most fragile of creatures. Your toughness is that of an insect; you have the insect's resistant carapace; but all one would have to do would be to bear down on it a little hard. . . . But no, I shall not bear down on it.

Besides, I am boasting. One never really knows anyone. What is actually left of you once that last mask that Nietzsche mentions is tossed aside? Those who love you do not love the real you; those who hate you do not hate the real you; what they love and hate is a rope-dancer. Still, the other evening at Marigny, I felt that I was suffering for the real Cocteau, the invisible Cocteau, the Cocteau that nobody knows, but that God knows and loves.

Because we are loved. That is the basis of everything. Also, it is something you have never understood, I think, even at the moment of your conversion. Christianity believes whole-heartedly in the unbelievable tidings that man is loved by his Creator, and, what is still more astonishing, that wretched though man be, he is capable of loving his Creator back. How strange it is, when one thinks of it, to love the Infinite Being and to call the Infinite Being "Our Father!" Some people must have felt in debt to you for a very bitter joy, at that moment in your play when the Our Father becomes a pretext for buffoonery, and a little later, when Jean Desailly utters an unclean little speech about the Eucharist—the joy of feeling that your arrow, piercing through the heart of Christ, goes on to strike their own hearts. I have always loved the cry of Clovis, that barbarian and savage, to whom Saint Remi was relating the story of the Passion: "If only I had been there with my Franks!" We were there, at Marigny, but what could we do, what could I do, I, who no longer have a voice with which to cry out? What could I do but leave? The only other thing I can do is to write you. If I kept silent any longer, the very stones would cry out.

No, do not allege to me, as you do in your program, that the remarks of your characters are not to be taken as representing your own thoughts. "Jean Cocteau has always sought to stress the chasm existing between himself and his work" writes a naive editor of *Match*, who is merely repeating his lesson like a parrot. "He speaks of it as though it were something foreign to him." I can imagine pupil Cocteau protesting: "No, teacher, I didn't do it!" But he still holds a spitball in his hand.

Essentially, Jean Desailly is your mouthpiece. Don't try to deny it; when he speaks it is you who are speaking. At times, Desailly slips out of his role and turns into Jean Cocteau in actual life. He plays the Coctian role. *Bacchus* shows us Jean Cocteau under the influence of Sartre, the same Cocteau that we knew in 1910 bathed by the last fires of Rostand; but even then he was finishing dancing his *Danse de Sophocle* with his eye set on Anna de Noailles. Even then Diaghilev, Satie, Picasso, Gide, Apollinaire, Max Jacob and other major planets were drawing this roguish satellite into their orbits.

Forty years have elapsed. We are now in the era of "God is dead." This idea is in the air, and you have spent your whole life chasing air-currents. Now or never is the moment, isn't it, to settle accounts with this corpse, and still more with this tiresome, drivelling old Church which obstinately persists in trying to frighten us by telling us tales of the other world, this Church which, long after we have left it, still succeeds in tempering our pleasure, which does not tire of writing with the gnarled fingers of her shrivelled hand on the wall of the festive banquet hall the Name which is above all names. Cocteau the child stamps his foot: "There is no Hell! There is no Hell!" There is no Hell, since there will be no Judgment, and there will be no Judgment because there is no God. Sartre proved it after many others had already proved it, and they were by no means the first to do so. Sartre, so the papers tell us, was seated in the midst of the crowd, jubilantly watching Cocteau tieing his old Mother to the pillar at Marigny and scoffing at Her for three hours.

Yes, of course I understand: it is the Church of the Renaissance that you are talking about, the paganized Church, the simoniacal Church for which Luther's heresy was a just punishment. You could have denounced its shameful deeds without disturbing me in the least. When Bernanos unleashed himself (and with what violence!) against the Spanish episcopate during the civil war, it didn't occur to anyone that he was attacking Holy Church. The most furious pamphleteers, like Léon Bloy, never touched the mystery of the Church. I myself, in *La Pierre d'achoppement,* said everything I felt about certain abuses. Was anyone shocked? A friend who is dear to both of us, Jacques Maritain, wrote that the Church is holy, but its members are sinners. You could have let yourself go to your heart's content against these rotten members, and you wouldn't have seriously offended any of us. All that was needed in your play was the presence of a single authentic saint, or even of one true Christian. Do you really believe that holiness had vanished from the earth in the sixteenth century? Have you never heard of Theresa of Avila, Luther's younger sister, but by not many years, or of Saint John of the Cross? Do you think the Counter-Reformation would have been possible if the stream of holiness in the Church had been interrupted for a single minute?

Yes, even in Germany there was no lack in the sixteenth century of men like Father Charles, the son of Charles de Foucauld, a truer angel than those you invented, and of one of whom you wrote that he was "prayer turned into man."

But you chose to make the Church incarnate in the person of a clown of a bishop and that of a political cardinal, the latter in my opinion worse than the clown. Through them, your mockery strikes at the very soul of the Church. If I had the text of your play at my disposal, I would bring out by direct quotations what there is that is shocking in your sneering at holy things—such sneering as atheists, who do not know The One they deny, are not capable of. A journalist was surprised that I reacted so violently to *Bacchus* when Sartre's play had left me cold. It is a fact that I was not shocked by *Le Diable et le bon Dieu.* An atheist laboriously carries to the stage the reasons for his unbelief. From him we cannot expect anything else; what else could he give us? We can only repeat about him Pascal's words: "They blaspheme what they do not know." All of Sartre's arrows go wild in an empty sky; whom can they strike, considering that there is no one there? I may add that Sartre only seems to treat things lightly. He treats serious things seriously. To say that he and I are not friends is an understatement; yet, when I mention his play and yours in the same breath, I feel that I am doing him an injustice. This is not at all a literary judgment. I leave it to others to pass on the literary merits of *Bacchus*. All I want to say is that Sartre the playwright develops his problem and brings it to life with material that he arranges according to his own lights. Sartre does not deny anybody. To speak his language, Sartre is not a slut. Neither are you, to be sure. But this does not hinder you from following a tortuous, sly path as you go from cue to cue. You seek to discredit, to make ridiculous and hateful a Power by which you feel that you are judged at every step. And we are already judged, dear Jean. Our copy has already been collected.

Sartre has blazed the trail, and one can get through. Of course, one does not plagiarize ideas, so that is not your achievement. But your spite is authentic. How long you have held it back! Now you relieve yourself at one stroke. You come back twice to a definition of the Church the exact terms of which I did not note down, but according to which its mission is to dominate the human conscience. You accuse it of doing nothing but forbidding, threatening, and preventing poor living creatures from going around in a ring and fornicating in peace until they have reached satiety. You stress the medieval aspects of Hell. Stories of boiling oil visibly cheer you up.

Listen to me; in concluding, I should like to talk to you about Hell. Let us put images aside. Hell is a word, and who would be so bold as to say exactly what corresponds to it in eternity? Let us restrict ourselves to what we know here below, to what the teaching of the little catechism discusses concerning our daily reality and the most hidden and disguised parts of our lives. Evil exists; you know it, and we all know it. Good exists too, and you have seen its reflection on the countenances of Father Charles and Maritain. Gide, who was shrewder than both of us put together, tried in vain to make us believe, during half a century of literary output, that evil is good. Roger Martin du Gard, in the volume of recollections that he has just dedicated to him, quotes some amazing words of his, in which Gide alleges that the young creatures with whom he had dealings gained a great deal from their contacts with him: "I can say this in justice to myself: upon the young people who came to me, my influence has always been useful and wholesome. Yes, this is not a paradox: my role has always been that of a moralizer. . . ." One must read this whole page, in which he takes good care not to distinguish between those on whom he exerted only a spiritual influence and the others. . . . Don't you think that here the very excess of lying unmasks the Master of the Lie? (I am not referring to Gide when I say this.) Evil is evil.

You will grant me that our own lives as men of letters and that of Father Charles (I keep coming back to the saint you happen to know) do not have the same value; they have not borne the same kind of fruit; they will not have the same eternal duration. It is true that there exists a hidden saintliness in some sinful lives, and that Pharisaism coils itself secretly around some seemingly saintly qualities. I am the author of *La Pharisienne*, so you cannot teach me anything on this subject. But you will agree with me that one cannot confuse an existence completely devoted to the poor, to humble daily service, and to God, with a life devoted to self-gratification. I do not know what Hell is. But I do know that each one of us will one day be asked to account for his soul. I know that we can lose ourselves and lose our brothers, and that this loss consists in being eternally separated from eternal love. That is what the Church teaches, while at the same time she puts at our disposal that inexhaustible treasure known as the Communion of Saints. The period in Church history that you chose, because it is the spot of an old wound that it will always be easy to reopen and make bleed, is the sixteenth century. The fact that during that period some pompous Popes and some simoniacal priests turned into coin what they had received gratuitously, changes nothing in this mysterious economy of the reversibility that reigns in the realm of souls under the sign of the Redemption.

"La Femme-tronc!" The headless woman! You are very pleased with yourself for having coined this word with which to designate Holy Church. It is fine spittle indeed. Ah! There is something to laugh about, and as a matter of fact, all Paris laughed for a good long while, like Herod's court and Herod himself before the disfigured Lord: "No matter what you say, no one but Jean can coin words like these!" Yet, the priest who once, in a little house in Meudon, raised his hand above you while he pronounced the words that absolved you, asked nothing in return but a little repentance and a beginning of love; neither did the saint who gave you the living bread to eat, the living Christ, require gold or silver of you.

The priest knows neither who we are nor where we come from. Anyone, no matter who he is, can kneel before this Table, and the Lord comes.

"*La femme-tronc*"? Do you believe that she has in life the ignoble face that Pierre Bertin bestows upon her? No, she has that poor, pure face of a vicar of your parish, and it is he whom you have slapped without knowing it. She is the worker-priest of Montreuil. The "*femme-tronc*"? Every morning, in the habit of a little sister of the Assumption, she does the housework of the poor. The "headless woman" is also the woman with head winged in white, whom Saint Vincent de Paul gave to the sick of the earth. And who are you to rise against her? In 1926, you wrote Jacques Maritain: "I have lost my seven best friends. I might as well say that seven times God gave me Graces without my noticing it." Yes; and since then Jean Desbordes has died a hero's death, tortured by the Germans; Max Jacob has undergone martyrdom, and I pray to him for you and for me. And Maurice Sachs, who recited his prayer before your photograph, how did he die? Oh, Jean, who are we to act so brave against God?

The "headless woman": thus you denounce the Church of Saint Augustine, of Saint Thomas, of Saint Bonaventure, of Saint Francis, of Saint John of the Cross, of Saint Theresa, of Pascal. . . . The "*femme-tronc*"? After all, why not? The Church is the trunk of the poor, of whom you and I are a part. The trunk? Say rather the breast, where beats the heart that the lance laid bare. You drank at this spring, one morning in 1926, and the angels who surrounded you were not called Heurtebise, as in your *Orphée*. No matter how old you live to be, the day draws near when real angels will surround you again, summoned perhaps by Max Jacob, because the tight-rope on which you have been dancing forward for years will be disappearing in the shadows of death. May it be God's will that at that moment the *femme-tronc* may enter your room one last time, under the guise of a consecrated man to whom she has given her power to absolve: "At the hour of the *Christus venit,* at the crowing of the cock. . . ." The cock will crow, and against the heart of his Lord, Harlequin will weep bitterly!

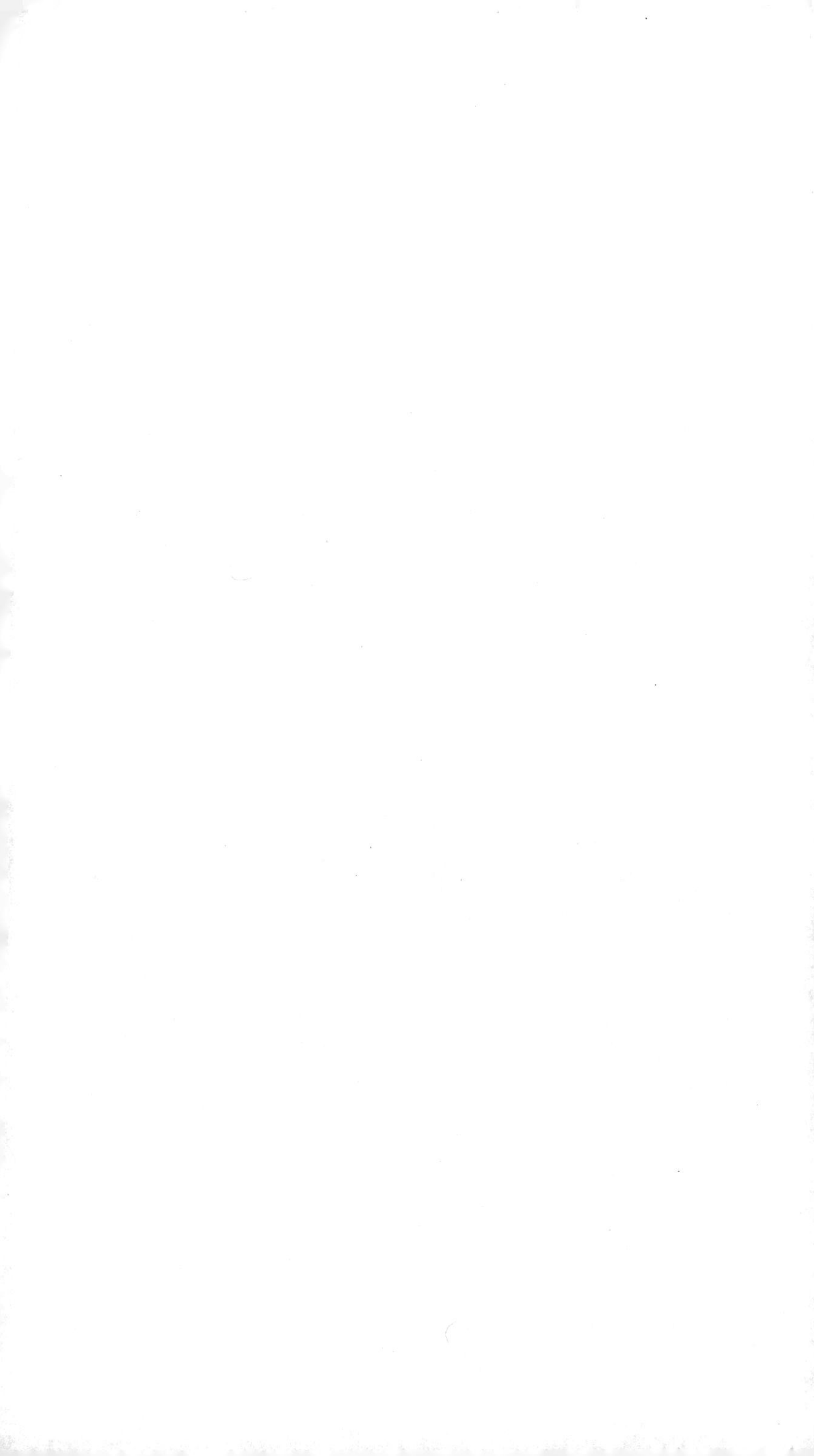

www.ingramcontent.com/pod-product-compliance
Lightning Source LLC
LaVergne TN
LVHW091007080826
845145LV00003B/1161
9780806529004